CONTENTS

HELLO...

IN THIS BOOK I AM GOING TO SHOW YOU HOW TO DRAW CARTOONS. EVEN IF YOU HAVE NEVER DRAWN ANYTHING BEFORE - YOU CAN DRAW CARTOONS. ONCE YOU HAVE LEARNED THE BASICS THERE WILL BE NO STOPPING YOU!

*ALL YOU NEED TO START IS A PENCIL AND SOME PAPER.

READY, SET, LET'S GO...

LET'S START WITH SOMETHING THAT MOST OF US WILL HAVE DRAWN AT SOME TIME...

... **STICK FIGURES!**

EVEN "REAL" ARTISTS WILL OFTEN START THEIR PAINTINGS WITH A STICK FIGURE SKETCH. IT HELPS THEM GET EVERYTHING IN ITS PLACE.

IN FACT, THE WORD '**CARTOON**' ORIGINALLY MEANT...

... **A QUICK SKETCH FOR AN OIL PAINTING!**

STICK FIGURES ARE REALLY EASY!

(1)

DRAW A LOLLIPOP SHAPE... THIS MAKES THE HEAD AND THE BACKBONE...

(2)

...NOW ADD THE HIPS AT THE BOTTOM OF THE BACKBONE AND SHOULDERS AT THE TOP...

(3)

...TWO ARMS NEXT- FIXED AT THE ENDS OF THE SHOULDERS...

(4)

NOW THE LEGS...

AND THAT'S IT!

YOUR VERY FIRST CARTOON!

* LEAVE OFF THE HIP AND SHOULDER STICKS WHEN YOU DRAW A FIGURE FROM THE SIDE – BECAUSE YOU CAN'T SEE THEM. CHECK THIS IN A MIRROR!

WE WANT PLENTY OF ACTION IN OUR CARTOONS – SO LET'S DRAW OUR SIMPLE STICK FIGURES IN A VARIETY OF DIFFERENT POSES...

SOMEONE RUNNING WILL BE LEANING FORWARD, LIKE THIS.

SOMEONE SITTING IN A CHAIR WILL BE LEANING BACK.

PUSHING A SUPERMARKET TROLLY CAN BE HARD WORK...

KICKING A FOOTBALL IS ENERGETIC...

NOT TO MENTION DANCING A HIGHLAND FLING!

YOU CAN MAKE A **REAL** STICK FIGURE TO HELP WORK OUT SOME OF THESE POSES...

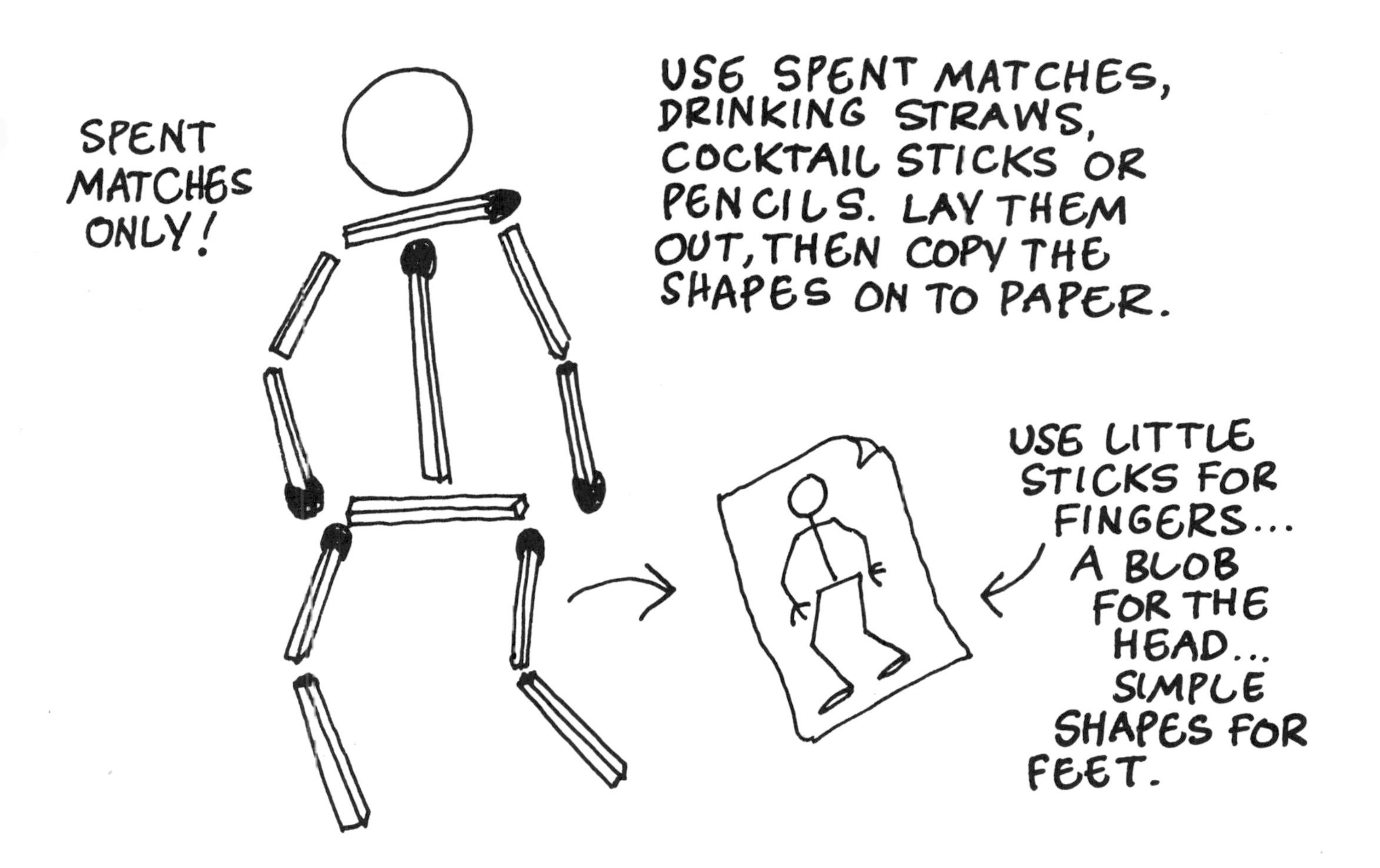

YOU CAN ALSO USE SHAPES FROM NEWSPAPERS...
USE TRACING PAPER TO COPY FROM PHOTOGRAPHS.

THERE IS NOTHING TO STOP YOU MAKING ODD SHAPES WITH YOUR STICK FIGURES...
YOU DON'T HAVE TO KEEP TO "NORMAL" PROPORTIONS.

NOW YOU CAN START DRAWING YOUR VERY OWN CARTOONS USING THESE SIMPLE STICK FIGURES...

YOU CAN EVEN DRAW SIMPLE STRIP CARTOONS...

SPEND SOME TIME PRACTISING THESE BASIC STICK FIGURES - THEY WILL HELP YOU TO DRAW GOOD, ACTION PACKED CARTOONS!
WE'LL HAVE A BREAK FROM STICK FIGURES NOW. IN THE NEXT SECTION WE WILL LEARN TO DRAW...

FUNNY FACES!

"I'M TAKING THIS AWAY FROM YOU BEFORE YOU HAVE ANY MORE CRAZY IDEAS...
DOCTOR FRANKENSTEIN!"

DRAWING FUNNY FACES...

NOW THAT WE HAVE OUR STICK FIGURES 'UP AND RUNNING' IT'S TIME TO GIVE THEM PERSONALITIES OF THEIR OWN...

...THE FACES IN CARTOONS ARE IMPORTANT. THEY CONVEY THE EMOTIONS YOUR CHARACTERS ARE FEELING.

...COPY MY FACES TO BEGIN WITH - YOU WILL SOON DEVELOP YOUR OWN.

DRAW THESE FACES IN SIMPLE OVAL SHAPES - WITH AN UPSIDE DOWN QUESTION MARK FOR A NOSE, AND THE NUMBER '3' FOR EARS.

IN A SURPRISED FACE THE EYES ARE DRAWN WIDE OPEN, WITH THE EYEBROWS HIGH IN THE FOREHEAD. THE MOUTH IS JUST A LITTLE DOT.

IN A CONTENTED FACE THE EYES AND MOUTH ARE SIMPLE CURVES - FACING UPWARDS.

* WE ALSO USE THIS FACE FOR SOMEONE WHO IS PROUD.

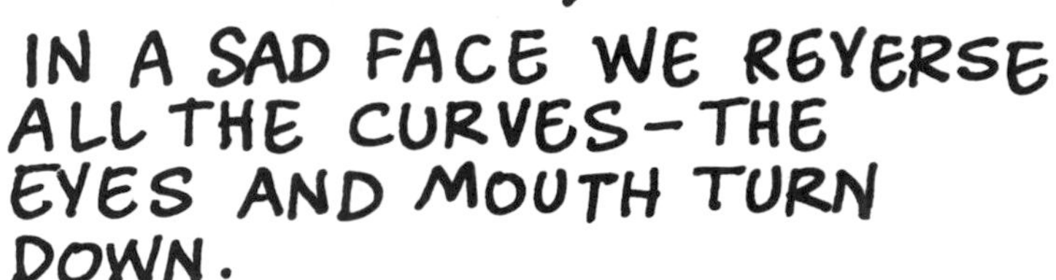

IN A SAD FACE WE REVERSE ALL THE CURVES - THE EYES AND MOUTH TURN DOWN.

* MAKE A POINT OF LOOKING AT LOTS OF CARTOONS TO SEE HOW THE DIFFERENT FACES ARE DRAWN!

IF WE USE THE EYES FROM THE SURPRISED FACE AND THE MOUTH FROM THE CONTENTED FACE WE HAVE A... HAPPY FACE...

... MAKE THE SMILE BIGGER - COMPLETE WITH TEETH - AND YOU HAVE A LOTTERY WINNER

AN ANGRY FACE LOOKS OUT FROM UNDER THESE DOWN POINTING EYEBROWS...
... COMPLETE WITH BARED TEETH!

A SICK FACE HAS SAD EYES - AND A WIGGLY MOUTH.

* HAVE THE TONGUE STICKING OUT, OR A THERMOMETER, TO SHOW ILLNESS.

HE MUST BE THE LOTTERY LOSER!

*
WE HAVE NOW DRAWN THE SIX MOST COMMON FACES YOU WILL FIND IN CARTOONS.

ONCE YOU HAVE LEARNED THESE BASIC EXPRESSIONS YOU CAN CREATE NEW ONES OF YOUR OWN...

YOU CAN CREATE ANY NUMBER OF FACES BY COMBINING THE FEATURES YOU ALREADY KNOW...

PLOTTING REVENGE

ANGRY EYES + HAPPY MOUTH

MAKING THE BEST OF IT

HAPPY EYES + SAD MOUTH

OOPS!

SAD EYES + SURPRISED MOUTH

LEARN TO DRAW FACES FROM THE SIDE AS WELL AS THE FRONT...

...USE THE SAME SHAPE FOR THE NOSE...

...DRAW HALF THE MOUTH...

...MAKE THE EYE FURTHEST FROM YOU A BIT SMALLER.

DRAW YOUR OWN FACE WITH A MIRROR...

* ON THE NEXT PAGE WE'LL SEE HOW TO MAKE THESE FACES INTO MEN AND WOMEN.

IT'S EASY TO MAKE THESE SIMPLE FACES INTO MALE OR FEMALE CARTOON CHARACTERS...

WOMEN CAN HAVE LONG EYELASHES AND LIPSTICK... AND OFTEN HAVE MORE HAIR THAN MEN!

MEN CAN BE STUBBLY, WITH SHORT HAIR - OR EVEN NONE AT ALL!

DRAW A FEW SIMPLE FACES AND HAVE A GO...

* PICK UP YOUR PENCIL AND TRY IT!

SOME FACES CAN EITHER BE MALE OR FEMALE...

... LIKE THIS ONE

AS WELL AS BEING MALE OR FEMALE, YOUR CARTOON PEOPLE CAN BE YOUNG AND OLD...

... OLDIES - LIKE ME - OFTEN HAVE WRINKLES - AND MIGHT BE A LITTLE MORE STOOPED... THEY WILL ALSO DRESS IN A MORE CONSERVATIVE WAY. (NORMALLY!)

IT'S ALSO LOTS OF FUN DRAWING YOUNG PEOPLE. THEY ARE THE ONES MOST LIKELY TO DRESS IN A CRAZY WAY TO BEGIN WITH!

VERY YOUNG CHILDREN HAVE LARGE HEADS AND SMALL BODIES.

YOU CAN – IF YOU WANT – ADD LOTS OF **DETAIL** TO YOUR CARTOONS...

... BEARDS AND MOUSTACHES
... SPECTACLES, HATS,
... PORTABLE STEREOS, ETC, ETC!

* OF COURSE, YOUR CARTOON CHARACTER DOESN'T HAVE TO BE A PERSON...

. . . ARE LOTS OF FUN TO DRAW AND APPEAL TO ALMOST EVERYONE. EITHER SOFT AND CUDDLY, OR PLENTY OF WHISKERS, FUR AND SHARP TEETH . . . !

* AS WELL AS ANIMALS, WHY NOT TRY SOME TALKING SHOES – A SINGING CAMERA OR A COMPUTER THAT TYPES YOUR LETTERS FOR YOU ?

NOW YOU CAN COMBINE THE **FUNNY FACES** WITH THE STICK FIGURES FROM THE LAST SECTION...

....YOUR CARTOONS WILL REALLY START TO COME TO LIFE NOW!

...AND I'M NOT COMING OUT UNTIL YOU LEARN TO DRAW
CLOTHES!
BATH

SO FAR WE HAVE ONLY BEEN DRAWING IN PENCIL; AS YOU BECOME MORE CONFIDENT YOU WILL WANT TO MAKE YOUR DRAWING MORE PERMANENT.

THIS IS WHAT I USE ...

PENCIL - USED FOR GENERAL SKETCHING AND ROUGH LAYOUTS. A GRADE 'B' IS EASY TO RUB OUT.

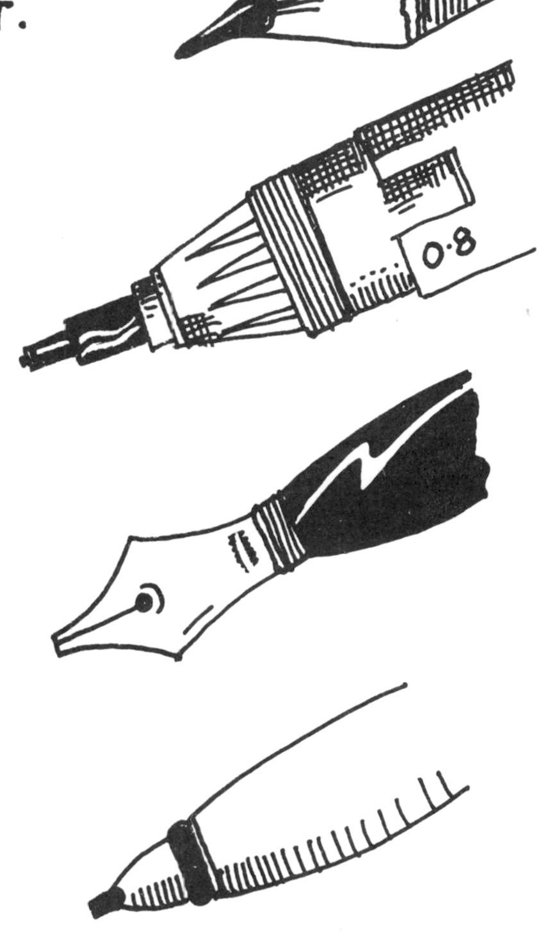

TECHNICAL PEN - GIVES A VERY EVEN AND PRECISE LINE. THIS BOOK WAS DRAWN AND LETTERED WITH A TECHNICAL PEN!

FOUNTAIN PEN - USE A WATER BASED INK IN A FOUNTAIN PEN OR IT MAY CLOG. OLD 'DIP' PENS ARE ALSO FUN TO EXPERIMENT WITH.

FELT-TIPPED PENS - ARE CHEAP AND EASY TO REFILL. THE INK CAN FADE IN TIME, SO USE FOR SKETCHES ONLY!

*

I USUALLY DRAW MY CARTOONS IN PENCIL FIRST. THEN I DRAW OVER IT WITH A TECHNICAL PEN. WHEN THE INK IS COMPLETELY DRY I RUB OUT THE PENCIL LINES.

SOME CARTOONISTS DRAW WITH A BRUSH - YOU COULD TRY THIS YOURSELF.

TO KEEP YOUR PENCILS AT THEIR BEST YOU WILL NEED A PENCIL SHARPENER.

A SOFT RUBBER WILL REMOVE UNWANTED PENCIL LINES WITHOUT DAMAGING THE PAPER.

COVER UP SMALL MISTAKES WITH TYPEWRITER CORRECTION FLUID.

COVER UP LARGER MISTAKES WITH A 'GLUED ON' PATCH OF PAPER - THEN SIMPLY REDRAW OVER THIS.

* IT'S O.K. - LOTS OF FAMOUS CARTOONISTS HAVE TO PATCH AND CORRECT!

* SEE HOW I HAVE MADE THESE TWO CHARACTERS DIFFERENT.
* NOTE THE FACIAL EXPRESSIONS..
* IF YOU HAVE PROBLEMS DRAWING HANDS~ PUT THEM IN POCKETS. (WE WILL LEARN TO DRAW HANDS IN A FEW PAGES TIME.)
"WORST OF ALL-I HAVE TO STEER THE CAR WITH MY KNEES WHEN I WANT TO USE THE MOBILE 'PHONE!"
* I HAVE USED SIMPLE SHAPES FOR HANDS AND CLOTHES.

....AND NOW→LET'S LEARN TO DRAW...

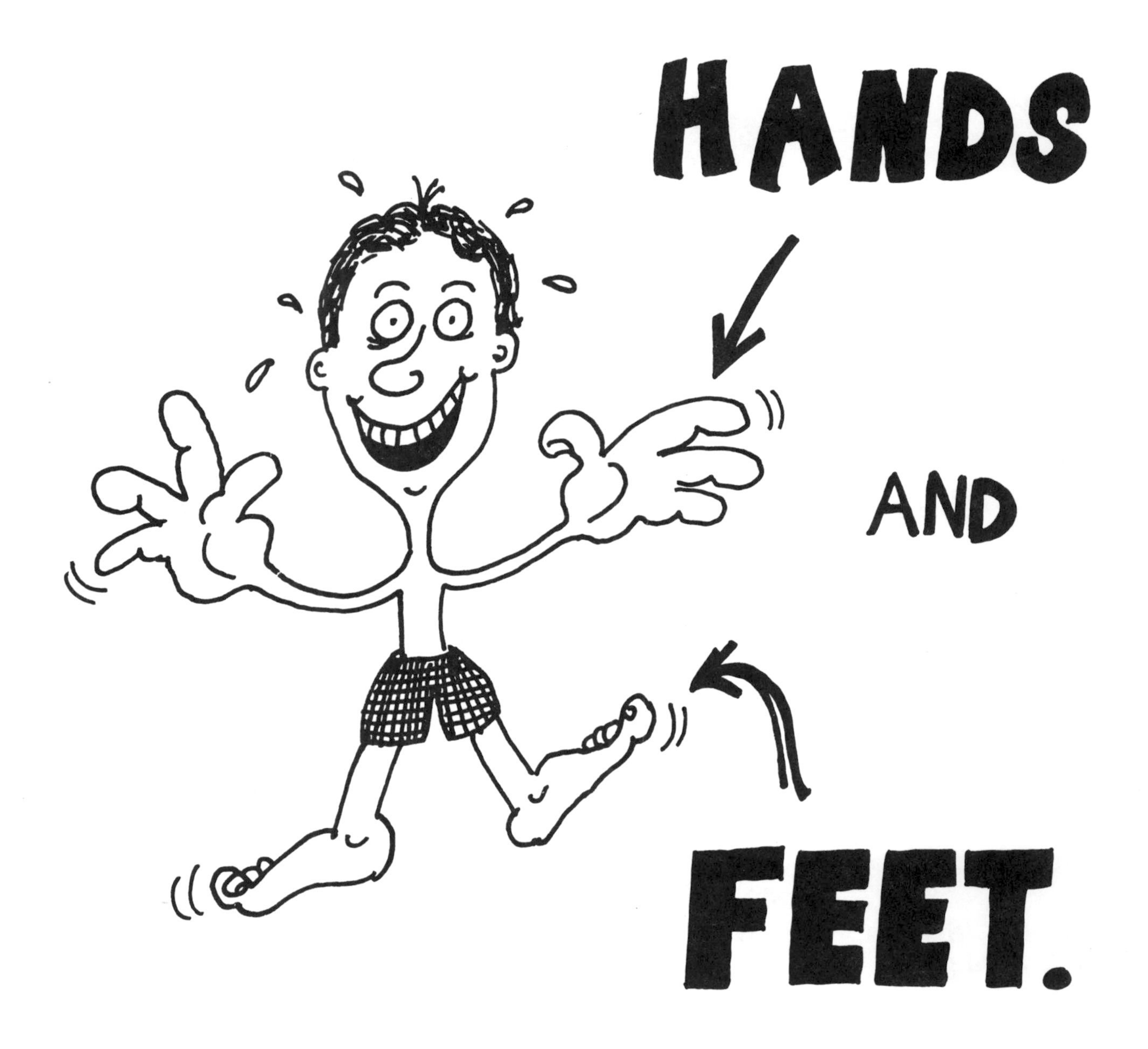

* YOU CAN HAVE EVEN MORE FUN WITH YOUR CARTOON CHARACTERS ONCE THEY HAVE HANDS AND FEET.
OVER THE NEXT FEW PAGES I WILL SHOW YOU SOME SIMPLE WAYS TO DRAW THESE ESSENTIAL EXTREMITIES...

...NOW... BEST **FEET** FORWARD...

START OUT BY DRAWING REALLY SIMPLE SHAPES FOR FEET – LIKE THESE...

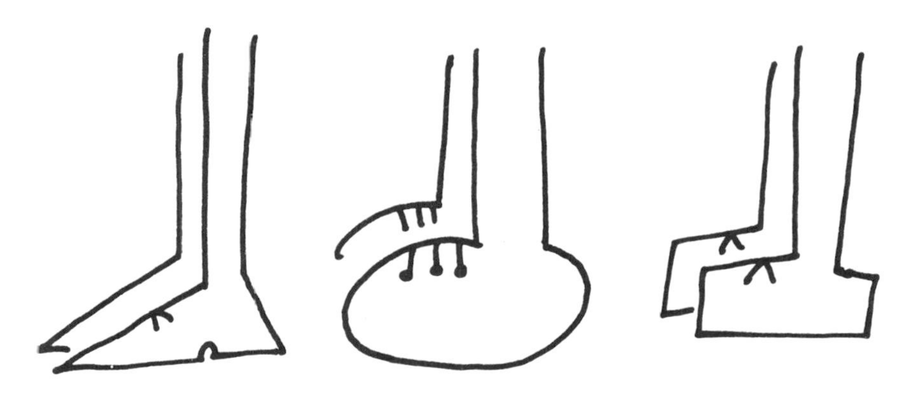

ALWAYS DRAW SOME SORT OF **HEEL** SHAPE AT THE BACK – IT HELPS TO BALANCE THE FOOT.

EXPERIMENT WITH BARE FEET, BOOTS, SHOES, SLIPPERS, CLAWS ?! * ?

MEN...

MAINLY WEAR FLAT-SOLED SHOES AND BOOTS.

THEY OFTEN HAVE HAIRY FEET.

TRY DRAWING SLIPPERS, WELLIES, SANDALS, HIKING BOOTS AND CRAZY TRAINERS!

WOMEN...

...OFTEN WEAR A WIDER VARIETY OF MUCH MORE INTERESTING FOOTWEAR.

...EVERYTHING THAT MEN WEAR PLUS HIGH HEELS, SLINKY BOOTS AND FURRY SLIPPERS.

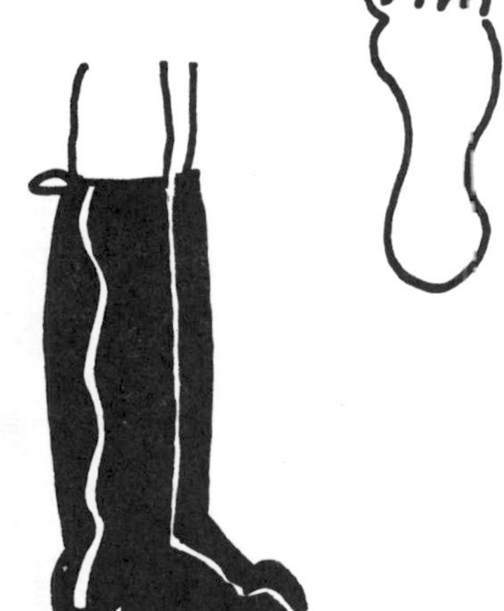

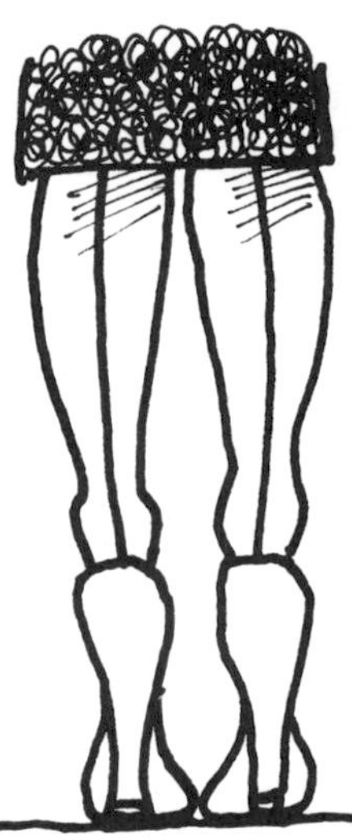

NOW - LET'S ADD SOME FEET AND SHOES TO OUR STICK FIGURES.
* PRACTISE A FEW OF THESE - BUILD YOUR CONFIDENCE!
YIKE! TRAINERS

✱ IN THESE CARTOONS THE HANDS PLAY AN IMPORTANT PART IN MAKING THE JOKE –

SO – TURN THE PAGE AND WE'LL LEARN HOW TO DRAW THEM !

HANDS ARE IMPORTANT IN CARTOONS.

THEY CAN GRIP, POINT, SQUEEZE, WAVE, THREATEN, THROW AND MUCH, MUCH MORE!

A SIMPLE HAND CAN BE DRAWN QUICKLY - LIKE A BUNCH OF BANANAS.

KEEP THE SHAPES SIMPLE AND DON'T WORRY ABOUT DETAILS.

*FINGERS CAN BE ROUNDED OR SHARP, WRINKLED OR SMOOTH...

DON'T BOTHER WITH FINGERNAILS...

CARTOON HANDS CAN BE DRAWN WITH 3 FINGERS OR WITH 4 FINGERS – PICK THE ONE THAT SUITS YOU BEST!

* TO GET THE THUMB IN THE RIGHT PLACE CHECK IN A MIRROR AS YOU DRAW.

* MAKE THE HAND AS BIG AS YOU LIKE....

OUR CARTOON FIGURE IS ALMOST COMPLETE...

...ALL WE HAVE TO DO NOW IS DRESS IT UP!

YOU'VE BEEN WORKING HARD! HERE'S A 'CARTOON BREAK' BEFORE WE MOVE ON TO THE NEXT SECTION...

" THEY NEED A DOUBLE ACT - CAN YOU CALL THE POT?! "

* AS I SAID EARLIER, YOUR CARTOONS CAN BE ABOUT ANYTHING - EVEN KETTLES!

THE CLOTHES SHOW...

BEGIN WITH THE USUAL STICK FIGURE – DRAWN IN SOFT PENCIL. A GRADE 'B' OR '2B' WILL ALLOW US TO RUB OUT THE PENCIL LINES EASILY WHEN THEY HAVE SERVED THEIR PURPOSE.

OVER THE STICK FIGURE CONSTRUCT A MORE ROUNDED FORM – USING 'BLOBS' FOR THE BODY AND TUBES FOR THE ARMS AND LEGS.

ON THIS SIDE IS THE COMPLETED CARTOON FIGURE.

*ON THIS SIDE YOU CAN SEE THE 'BLOBS' AND 'TUBES' I USED TO HELP ME CONSTRUCT THIS FIGURE

* COVER UP EACH SIDE WITH YOUR HAND TO SEE HOW ONE LEADS TO THE OTHER.

YOU CAN TRACE 'BLOB AND TUBE' FIGURES FROM NEWSPAPERS AND PHOTOGRAPHS AS WELL AS MAKING THEM FROM YOUR MATCHSTICK FIGURES.

EXPERIMENT WITH DIFFERENT PROPORTIONS...

→ KEEP A SMALL SKETCHPAD OR NOTEBOOK HANDY SO YOU CAN PRACTISE YOUR DRAWING WHENEVER THE MOOD TAKES YOU!

TRY DRAWING **MEN** IN SUITS, SHIRTS AND TIES, WOOLLY JUMPERS, HIKING GEAR, SCUBA DIVING SUITS, SWEATSHIRTS...

* COLLECT PICTURES FROM MAGAZINES FOR IDEAS.

THE CLOTHING CAN BE PART OF THE CARTOON TOO! A SHIRT CAN FIT A LITTLE TOO SNUGLY, OR BE MORE THAN A LITTLE ON THE BAGGY SIDE!

WOMEN CAN – OF COURSE – WEAR ALL THE THINGS THAT MEN CAN, PLUS SKIRTS AND DRESSES TOO!

* DON'T WORRY ABOUT DRAWING 'PROPER' ARMS AND LEGS – JUST DRAW STICK SHAPES FOR NOW.

OF COURSE YOU DON'T HAVE TO STICK RIGIDLY TO ANY OF THESE CATEGORIES...

...JUST DO YOUR OWN THING!

* KEEP YOUR EYES OPEN FOR CHANGING STYLES AND FASHIONS – ESPECIALLY IF YOU ARE DRAWING YOUNG PEOPLE...

*REMEMBER AS WELL ALL THOSE LITTLE EXTRAS THAT PEOPLE CARRY AROUND...

* SOME PEOPLE WEAR A UNIFORM...

* BUILD UP A COLLECTION OF DRAWINGS FOR FUTURE REFERENCE.

LET YOUR CARTOONS SET YOU FREE!

* YOU DON'T **HAVE** TO DRAW **CARTOONS** ABOUT THE **PRESENT DAY** – YOU CAN SETTLE IN ANY PLACE AND ANY TIME **YOU CHOOSE!**

* YOU CAN SET YOUR CARTOONS ON **ANOTHER PLANET** IF **YOU** WANT TO...

→ LET YOUR IMAGINATION RUN WILD... WHY NOT?!*

ONE OF MY FIRST CARTOON STRIPS WAS SET IN THE...

GARDEN OF EDEN!

* WHY NOT TRY OUT YOUR FAVOURITE PERIOD IN HISTORY...

...FROM CAVE MEN (AND WOMEN) TO COMPUTERS - FROM STONEHENGE TO THE SPACE SHUTTLE.

- **GO FOR IT!**

* YOU ALSO HAVE THE WORLD OF THE IMAGINARY TO HAVE FUN WITH!

IF THEY CAN MAKE A WOMAN FROM A MAN'S RIB....

BACKGROUNDS

HERE IS A DRAWING OF **ME** IN MY USUAL LOCATION...

* I HAVEN'T INCLUDED EVERY SINGLE THING FROM MY STUDIO IN MY DRAWING – JUST ENOUGH TO SHOW WHERE I AM – BUT NOT SO MUCH THAT THE DRAWING BECOMES CLUTTERED.

MAKE A NOTE OF THE THINGS YOU SEE IN A PARTICULAR PLACE, THEN DRAW 3 OR 4 OF THEM...

... IT'S SURPRISING JUST HOW LITTLE YOU NEED TO SEE IN A DRAWING TO TELL YOU WHERE YOU ARE...

... USING THE COLLECTION OF SKETCHES ABOVE I MADE UP THIS PUB SCENE

*TRY IT YOURSELF!

* **SPEND A FEW MINUTES** SKETCHING "EVERYDAY" OBJECTS AS YOU MOVE FROM ONE PLACE TO ANOTHER.

NOTE DOWN ANY DETAILS THAT INTEREST YOU!

...THIS WAY YOUR SKETCHBOOK WILL BE FULL OF POTENTIAL IDEAS -**PLUS**- YOU WILL BE GETTING IN PLENTY OF DRAWING PRACTISE!

(BETTER THAN GETTING SQUARE EYES WATCHING TELEVISION)

* BEGIN BY SKETCHING THE THINGS YOU FIND IN ALL THE DIFFERENT ROOMS IN YOUR OWN HOME...

TELEVISION
VIDEO
PLANTS
BOOKS
LIGHTS
ETC,
ETC...

* **HERE ARE** ANOTHER TWO EXAMPLES...

...SEE HOW **LITTLE** YOU ACTUALLY NEED TO DRAW TO SET THE SCENE...

...PEOPLE IN UNIFORM ARE VERY USEFUL CLUES TO TELL THE "VIEWER" WHERE THE CARTOON IS SET.

* MANY 'PROFESSIONAL' PEOPLE...

... DOCTORS
DENTISTS
ARCHITECTS
ETC...

...DISPLAY THEIR CERTIFICATES IN FRAMES...

... THIS IS ANOTHER GOOD 'CLUE' YOU CAN INCLUDE IN YOUR CARTOON.

YOU CAN HAVE A LOT OF FUN EXPERIMENTING WITH **DIFFERENT VIEWPOINTS**...

... LOOKING FROM BELOW THINGS APPEAR AS IF THE VIEWER WAS A CHILD OR SMALL ANIMAL- OR SOMEONE LYING DOWN-WHICH IS THE BEST WAY TO SKETCH IT!

* LOOKING FROM ABOVE THE OPPOSITE HAPPENS- YOU GET A 'BIRDS EYE VIEW' OF THE WORLD.

→ STAND ON A CHAIR AND SEE FOR YOURSELF!

* LIGHTLY PENCIL IN A TRIANGLE SHAPE TO BEGIN WITH, AND DRAW INSIDE IT.

WELL DONE!
YOU'VE REACHED THE END OF ANOTHER GRUELLING "CHAPTER"...
...HAVE A QUICK CARTOON BREAK!
THANK GOODNESS I'M STILL SINGLE...
LOVER LEA
IT'S SATELLITE T.V....

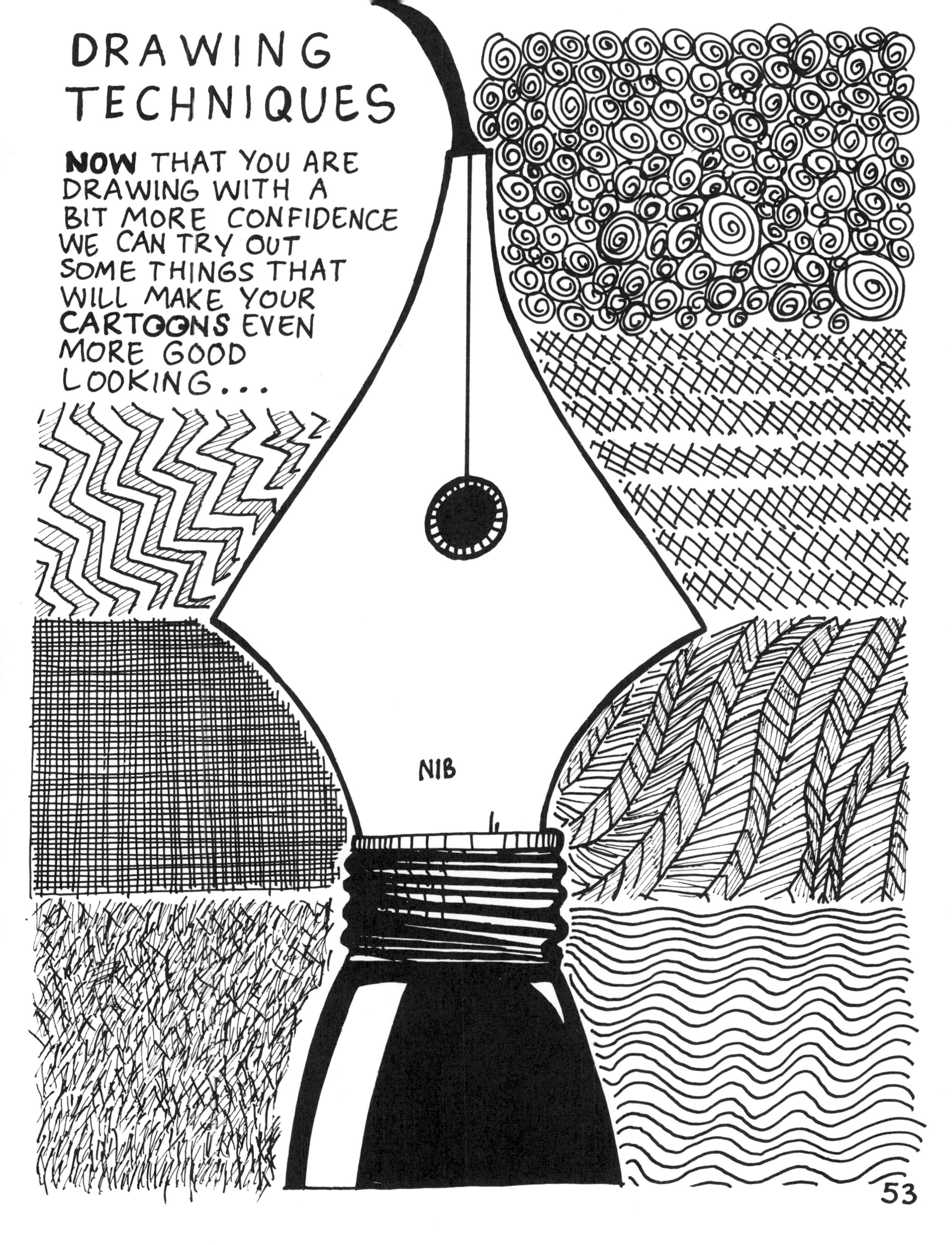
DRAWING TECHNIQUES
NOW THAT YOU ARE DRAWING WITH A BIT MORE CONFIDENCE WE CAN TRY OUT SOME THINGS THAT WILL MAKE YOUR CARTOONS EVEN MORE GOOD LOOKING...
NIB

USE AREAS OF SOLID BLACK IN YOUR CARTOONS TO MAKE THEM STRONGER...
...IT CAN ALSO BE USED TO MAKE LIGHTER AREAS MORE IMPORTANT.

* USE **BLACK** INDIAN INK - APPLIED WITH A SIZE 3 OR 4 ARTISTS' BRUSH.

(WASH THE BRUSH OUT IN WARM, SOAPY WATER AFTER USE.)

* SOME CARTOONISTS ONLY EVER DRAW WITH **A BRUSH** - NEVER A PEN.

* FOR A COMPLETE CHANGE TRY DRAWING IN WHITE ON A BLACK BACKGROUND...

...TYPEWRITER CORRECTION FLUID WORKS WELL.

PATTERN + SHADING.

* ADDING PATTERNS, SHADING OR TONE TO YOUR CARTOONS WILL MAKE THEM LOOK MORE 'FINISHED' AND LESS SKETCHY...

...TRY SOME OF THE PATTERNS ON PAGE 53 TO START YOU OFF –

–THEN INVENT SOME OF YOUR OWN!

* THE PATTERN YOU DRAW ON THINGS CAN HAVE QUITE A DRAMATIC EFFECT–

BE CAREFUL !

* TRY TARTAN –HERRINGBONE – AND OTHERS!

* IN A CARTOON WHICH CONTAINS A LOT OF DETAIL YOU CAN MAKE THE IMPORTANT PARTS STAND OUT BY DRAWING THEM WITH A THICKER LINE...

... THIS IS A GOOD TECHNIQUE TO LEARN - YOU CAN USE IT A LOT.

* I USE A ·4 TECHNICAL PEN FOR THE FINE LINES...

* TRY DRAWING THIS THICKER LINE WITH A **SIZE 3 OR 4 BRUSH.**

* USE THE THINNER LINE TO ADD DETAILS -LIKE THE GIRL'S HAIR IN THE CARTOON ABOVE...

*YOU CAN -OF COURSE-
DRAW YOUR CARTOONS
WITH JUST ABOUT
ANYTHING THAT YOU
HAPPEN TO HAVE AROUND.
I'VE DRAWN THE TOP
PART OF THIS
FIGURE WITH A
TECHNICAL
PEN...
...THE
BACKGROUND
IS FINGERTIPS
DIPPED IN INDIAN
INK...
...THE NEXT SECTION
IS DRAWN WITH
A NUMBER 3
BRUSH...
...A HOME-MADE
QUILL PEN WAS
USED FOR THIS
PART OF THE
DRAWING - JUST
CUT THE END OF
THE QUILL INTO
A ROUGH PEN NIB
SHAPE...
...THE BOTTOM
PART WAS DRAWN
WITH A THICK
FELT-TIP PEN.
THE BACKGROUND
IS A SPONGE
DIPPED IN
INK...
...THE LEGS
ARE SHADED
WITH DOTS!

TIME...
FOR ANOTHER CARTOON BREAK...
WELL - OTHER BOSSES MARRY SECRETARIES!
* COMPARE THESE TWO CARTOONS...
...THE TOP ONE HAS PLENTY OF TONE + TEXTURE...
...THE BOTTOM ONE IS A SIMPLE LINE DRAWING.
... SO, I'M STUCK WITH THIS PONYTAIL FOR THE REST OF ETERNITY ?!

HOPEFULLY, BY NOW, YOU WILL BE FINDING THE **ACTUAL DRAWING** OF YOUR CARTOONS A BIT EASIER.

SO-NOW WE NEED A GOOD SUPPLY OF **JOKE** IDEAS TO GIVE US SOMETHING TO DRAW...

... BECAUSE YOU NEVER KNOW WHERE YOUR CARTOONS WILL END UP!

FAME

HA HA HA HA HA

* ON THE NEXT FEW PAGES I WILL SHOW YOU MY METHODS OF "JOKE PRODUCTION"...

... WHEN YOU'VE READ THIS SECTION WHY NOT HAVE A TRY YOURSELF!?

WHERE DO YOU GET YOUR IDEAS ?

* CARTOON IDEAS ARE ALL AROUND US...

  ... YOU HAVE TO LEARN TO "TUNE IN" YOUR MIND TO PICK THEM UP...

* LISTEN TO FUNNY RADIO PROGRAMMES.
* ASK FAMILY AND FRIENDS TO TELL YOU THEIR FAVOURITE JOKES.
* WATCH TELEVISION.

* TURN EXISTING JOKES ON THEIR HEADS - CHANGE THE CHARACTERS AROUND.

  USE COMMON THEMES OR SITUATIONS... THERE MUST BE THOUSANDS OF DESERT ISLAND CARTOONS!

THERE ARE OFTEN FUNNY 'SNIPPETS' IN NEWSPAPERS AND MAGAZINES...

... BUT WATCH OUT FOR THINGS HAPPENING BEHIND YOU WHILE YOU ARE READING!

* **WE ARE NEVER** VERY FAR FROM SIGNS AND NOTICES - WRITE A FEW OF YOUR OWN!

* **WRITE DOWN** THE **'PUNCHLINE'** TO A FAVOURITE JOKE OR CARTOON - THEN THINK UP YOUR OWN ORIGINAL DRAWING TO GO WITH IT.

* JUST DRAW A COUPLE OF CHARACTERS DOING SOMETHING - AND SEE IF AN IDEA SPRINGS TO MIND. I OFTEN WORK LIKE THIS WHEN I GET STUCK FOR IDEAS.

REMEMBER... IF YOU CAN HAVE ONE IDEA, YOU CAN HAVE TEN; AND IF YOU CAN HAVE TEN IDEAS YOU COULD PRETTY SOON HAVE **HUNDREDS!!**

CONTRASTS... CAN BE FUNNY.

... OLD AND NEW
... FAST AND SLOW
... SMALL AND LARGE.

* **LAUREL AND HARDY** WERE FUNNY EVEN BEFORE THEY SAID OR DID ANYTHING BECAUSE OF THE CONTRAST IN THEIR SIZE AND SHAPE.

* TALL AND SHORT
... WET AND DRY
... STRONG AND WEAK

* CONTRAST THE WAY THAT DIFFERENT CHARACTERS REACT IN A VARIETY OF SITUATIONS.

PEOPLE HAVE JOBS, HOBBIES AND LEISURE INTERESTS THAT SOMETIMES INVOLVE USING SPECIALIST EQUIPMENT AND TERMS OR 'JARGON'.

SOME OF THESE THINGS CAN BE USED IN CARTOONS...

* **IN SOME CARTOONS** THERE ARE THINGS WHICH ARE HIDDEN FROM ONE OR MORE OF THE CHARACTERS – THE JOKE IS IN THE FACT THAT YOU KNOW SOMETHING THAT PEOPLE IN THE CARTOON DON'T!

* SOMETIMES THE JOKE IS IN THE VERY END OF THE CAPTION OR 'PUNCHLINE'.

I THINK LOVE IS THE MOST IMPORTANT THING IN A RELATIONSHIP...

SO – I'VE DECIDED TO FALL IN LOVE WITH THE FIRST LOTTERY WINNER I MEET!

→ NOW, TRY A FEW OF THESE **'JOKE PRODUCTION'** IDEAS FOR YOURSELF...

CARTOON
TIME FOR ANOTHER...
BREAK!
18
4
18 HOLES IN ONE- AS USUAL!
FLAMIN' TOURISTS!
OFFICE PARTIES P.L.C.
IN
OUT
IN
OUT
SHAKE IT ALL ABOUT!

* **SOME CARTOONS** HAVE WORDS IN THEM - THERE ARE A VARIETY OF WAYS OF ADDING THESE WORDS TO YOUR DRAWING...

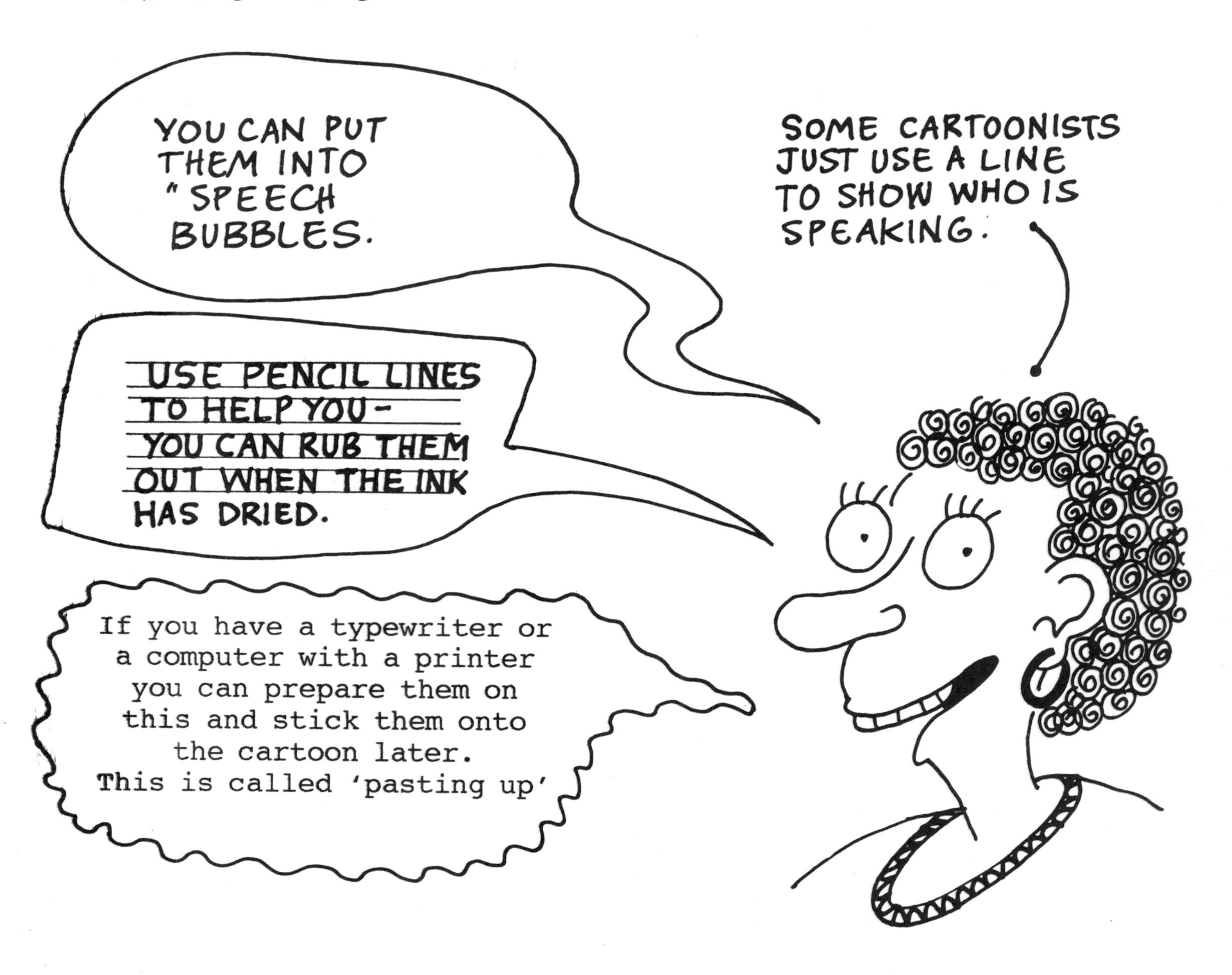

AS WELL AS SPEECH WE CAN ALSO ADD SOME OF THESE TO OUR **CARTOONS** . . .

* **ANGRY OR EXPLOSIVE** ACTIONS AND WORDS ARE SHOWN IN **SPIKY** SHAPES...

* DIRECTIONS – OR GENERAL INFORMATION FOR THE READER – IS USUALLY PUT INTO RECTANGLES, LIKE THIS...

→ NOT ALL CARTOONS HAVE WORDS IN THEM – SOME ARE PURELY "**VISUAL**" ...

* IN A '**VISUAL**' **CARTOON** WE RELY ON THE DRAWING TO TELL THE WHOLE STORY.

THIS STYLE OF CARTOON CAN BE QUITE DIFFICULT TO "GET INTO" AT FIRST- TRY INCORPORATING SOME **SIGNS** TO BEGIN WITH, LIKE THE ONES I HAVE USED IN THE **CARTOON** AT THE TOP OF THIS PAGE.

DRAWING **CARICATURES** CAN BE A LOT OF FUN, ESPECIALLY IF YOU HAVE A GIFT FOR IT!

* POLITICIANS, SUPERMODELS, ACTORS, ROYALS, MUSICIANS, ETC. ETC.

GET HOLD OF A **MIRROR** AND TRY IT OUT ON **YOURSELF** FIRST – OR WORK FROM **PHOTOS** OF FRIENDS AND FAMILY.

* THIS IS AN **EXAMPLE** OF HOW ONE OF MY CARTOONS LOOKS WHEN IT GOES OUT TO A NEWSPAPER OR MAGAZINE... ACTUAL SIZE! THE PRINTER WILL **REDUCE** IT TO THE SIZE REQUIRED BY THE MAGAZINE, LEAVING YOU FREE TO DRAW ANY SIZE YOU LIKE (**ALMOST!**).

You said take the baby to the park - you didn't say anything about bringing it back again...

* IF YOU'VE BEEN **WORKING HARD** YOUR CARTOONS WILL BE LOOKING PRETTY GOOD BY THIS STAGE.

MAYBE NOW IS THE TIME TO LET SOME OTHER PEOPLE ENJOY THEM...

➡ HERE ARE SOME IDEAS FOR THINGS YOU CAN DO WITH YOUR NEW-FOUND SKILLS...

* MAKE A FACE FOLDER!

TAKE A PIECE OF PAPER ABOUT
450mm BY 150mm.
FOLD IT INTO THREE EQUAL PARTS.
DRAW A FACE ON THE MIDDLE, THEN
FOLD EACH FLAP TO THE CENTRE AND
DRAW FACES ON THEM TOO.

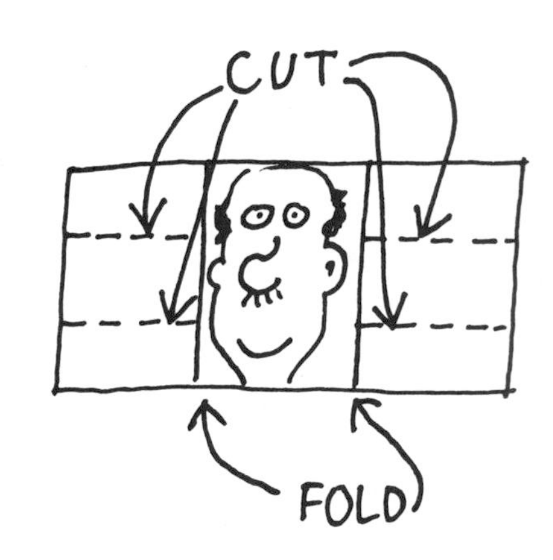

NOW CUT THE SIDE FLAPS INTO THREE STRIPS - EACH ONE 50mm WIDE.

NOW YOU CAN CREATE AN **AMAZING ASSORTMENT** OF FACES BY FOLDING AND UNFOLDING THE FLAPS.

* DRAW EYES IN THE TOP THIRD,
  NOSE AND EARS IN THE SECOND THIRD,
  MOUTH IN THE BOTTOM THIRD.

* MAKE THE FACES AS **VARIED** AS POSSIBLE.
  MIX UP MALE AND FEMALE FACES.
  ADD SOME **COLOUR** WITH PAINTS OR FELT PENS.